My Cursive
Handwriting Book

인생에
한 번쯤은

인생에
한 번쯤은 필기체로
영어 써보기

My Cursive
Handwriting Book

a b c d e f g h i j k l m n o p q r s t u v w x y z

small letters

A B C D E F G H I J K L M N O P Q R S T U V W X Y Z

capital letters

My Cursive Handwriting Book

인생에 한 번쯤은 필기체로 영어 써보기

초판 인쇄 2019년 11월 21일
발행 2019년 11월 28일

지 은 이 | 마샤영어개발연구원
펴 낸 이 | 양봉숙
디 자 인 | 김선희
편　　집 | 정효선
마 케 팅 | 이주철

펴 낸 곳 | 예스북
출판등록 | 제320-2005-25호 2005년 3월 21일
주　　소 | 서울시 마포구 서강로 131 신촌아이스페이스 1107호
전　　화 | (02)337-3054
팩　　스 | 0504-190-1001
E-mail | yesbooks@naver.com
홈페이지 | www.e-yesbook.co.kr

ISBN 978-89-92197-97-7 13740

My Cursive
Handwriting Book

인생에
한 번쯤은 필기체로
영어 써보기

예스북

이 책의 구성과 특징

속담속에서 만나는 단어 코너

◉ 알파벳 순서대로 대문자와
소문자를 쓰면서 익힙니다.

◉ 필기체 대문자와 소문자를 써보세요.

◉ 속담과 격언속에서 만나는 단어

animal 동물

animal   animal

◦ **Man is a social animal.**
인간은 사회적 동물이다.

Man is a social animal.

◉ 속담, 격언 속에 나오는 단어들을 통해 해당 알파벳을 집중 연습합니다.
속담, 격언을 그대로 쓰면서 그 뜻을 음미합니다.

명언 여행 코너

◉ **명언 여행**

◦ **Ask not what your country can do for you;**
ask what you can do for your country.
국가가 당신을 위해 무엇을 할 수 있는지 묻지 말고 당신이 국가를 위해 무엇을 할 수 있는지 물어보라.

Ask not what your country can do for you;

ask what you can do for your country.

◉ 앞에서는 짧은 문장을 써보았다면, 이제는 좀 더 긴 문장에 도전합니다.
가슴에 새겨지는 좋은 문장들로 엄선해서 구성했습니다.

● 나도 작가처럼

It was a bright cold day in April, and the clocks were striking thirteen. Winston Smith, his chin nuzzled into his breast in an effort to escape the vile wind, slipped quickly through the glass doors of Victory Mansions, though not quickly enough to prevent a swirl of gritty dust from entering along with him.

맑고 쌀쌀한 4월의 어느 날이었고, 시계는 13시를 알리고 있었다. 윈스턴 스미스는 차가운 바람을 피하느라고 턱 끝을 가슴에 틀어박고 빅토리 맨션의 유리문 안으로 잽싸게 들어갔다.
그렇지만 따라 들어오는 모래 먼지 회오리는 막을 수가 없었다.
(조지 오웰 '1984' - 첫 문장)

It was a bright cold day in April, and the clocks were working thirteen. Winston Smith, his chin nuzzled into his breast in an effort to escape the vile wind, slipped quickly through the glass doors of Victory Mansions, though not quickly enough to prevent a swirl of gritty dust from entering along with him.

● 문학작품 등에 나오는 유명한 문장들을 선보입니다.
긴 문장 쓰기를 통해 필기체에 자신감을 갖게 합니다.
해당 문장의 출처를 표시했습니다.

Capital letters
필기체 대문자

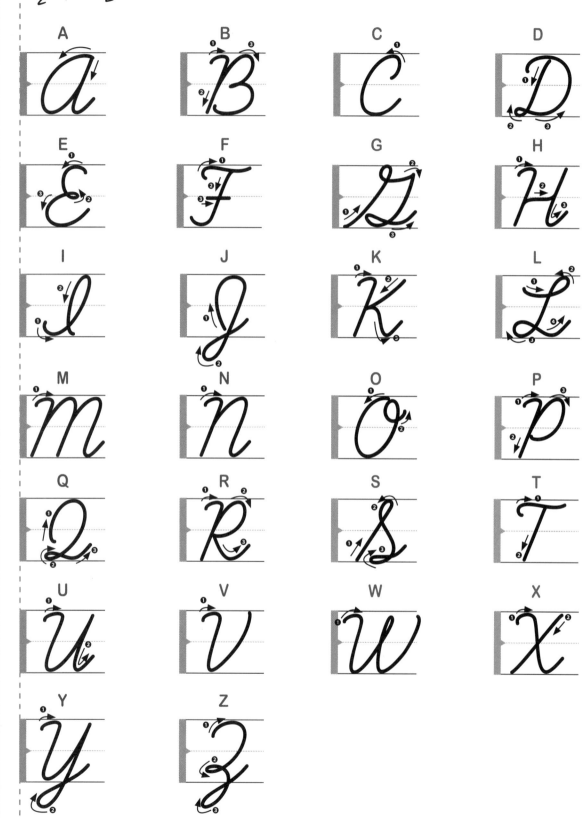

a

b

c

d

e

f

g

h

i

j

k

l

m

n

o

p

q

r

s

t

u

v

w

x

y

z

● 필기체 대문자를 써보세요.

A B C D E F G H I J K L M N O P Q R S T U V W X Y Z

A B C D E F G H I J K L M N O P Q R S T U V W X Y Z

● 필기체 소문자를 써보세요.

a b c d e f g h i j k l m n o p q r s t u v w x y z

a b c d e f g h i j k l m n o p q r s t u v w x y z

● 필기체 대문자를 이어서 써보세요.

ABCDEFGHIJKLMNOPQRSTUVWXYZ

ABCDEFGHIJKLMNOPQRSTUVWXYZ

● 필기체 소문자를 이어서 써보세요.

abcdefghijklmnopqrstuvwxyz

abcdefghijklmnopqrstuvwxyz

My Cursive Handwriting Book

필기체 대문자와 소문자를 써보세요.

A a a

a

a

a a

속담과 격언속에서 만나는 단어

animal 동물

animal animal

Man is a social animal.
인간은 사회적 동물이다.

Man is a social animal.

apple 사과

apple apple

An apple a day keeps the doctor away.
하루에 사과 하나면 의사를 멀리할 수 있다.

An apple a day keeps the doctor away.

art 예술

art art

Art is long, and life is short.
예술은 길고 인생은 짧다.

Art is long, and life is short.

ask 구하다

ask ask

Ask, and it shall be given to you.
구하라. 그러면 얻을 것이다.

Ask, and it shall be given to you.

attack 공격

attack attack

Attack is the best defense.
공격이 최선의 방어이다.

Attack is the best defense.

◉ 명언 여행

> **Ask not what your country can do for you;**
> **ask what you can do for your country.**
> 국가가 당신을 위해 무엇을 할 수 있는지 묻지 말고 당신이 국가를 위해 무엇을 할 수 있는지 물어보라.

Ask not what your country can do for you;

ask what you can do for your country.

> **No matter how humble it may be,**
> **there is no place like home.**
> 아무리 보잘것없다 할지라도, 집만 한 곳은 없다.

No matter how humble it may be,

there is no place like home.

> **A man is insensible to the relish of prosperity till he**
> **has tasted adversity.**
> 인간은 역경을 맛보기 전까지는 행복의 맛을 느끼지 못한다.

A man is insensible to the relish of prosperity till he

has tasted adversity.

● 나도 작가처럼

> It was a bright cold day in April, and the clocks were striking thirteen. Winston Smith, his chin nuzzled into his breast in an effort to escape the vile wind, slipped quickly through the glass doors of Victory Mansions, though not quickly enough to prevent a swirl of gritty dust from entering along with him.
>
> 맑고 쌀쌀한 4월의 어느 날이었고, 시계는 13시를 알리고 있었다. 윈스턴 스미스는 차가운 바람을 피하느라고 턱 끝을 가슴에 틀어박고 빅토리 맨션의 유리문 안으로 잽싸게 들어갔다. 그렇지만 따라 들어오는 모래 먼지 회오리는 막을 수가 없었다.
>
> (조지 오웰 '1984' - 첫 문장)

It was a bright cold day in April, and the clocks were striking thirteen. Winston Smith, his chin nuzzled into his breast in an effort to escape the vile wind, slipped quickly through the glass doors of Victory Mansions, though not quickly enough to prevent a swirl of gritty dust from entering along with him.

◉ 필기체 대문자와 소문자를 써보세요.

B _B_ _b_

B _b_

◉ 속담과 격언속에서 만나는 단어

barking 짖는

barking barking

A barking dog never bites.
짖는 개는 절대 물지 않는다.

A barking dog never bites.

basket 바구니

basket basket

Do not put all your eggs in one basket.
계란을 전부 한 바구니에 담지 말라.

Do not put all your eggs in one basket.

beginning 시작

beginning beginning

The beginning is half of the whole.
시작이 반이다.

The beginning is half of the whole.

beware 조심하다

beware beware

Beware of the wolf in sheep's clothing.
양가죽을 쓴 늑대를 조심하라.

Beware of the wolf in sheep's clothing.

bird 새

bird bird

Early bird catches the worm.
일찍 나는 새가 벌레를 잡는다.

Early bird catches the worm.

◉ 명언 여행

Body, soul, intelligence; to the body belong sensations, to the soul appetites, to the intelligence principles.
육신과, 영혼과, 지성 – 감각은 육신에 속하고 욕구는 영혼에 속하고 원칙들은 지성에 속한다.

Body, soul, intelligence; to the body belong sensations, to the soul appetites, to the intelligence principles.

The most beautiful thing in the world is, of course, the world itself.
세상에서 가장 아름다운 것은, 당연히, 세상 그 자체이다.

The most beautiful thing in the world is, of course, the world itself.

Prosperity makes friends, adversity tries them.
성공은 친구들을 만들고, 역경은 친구들을 시험한다.

Prosperity makes friends, adversity tries them.

● 나도 작가처럼

"Meaningless! Meaningless!" says the Teacher.
"Utterly meaningless! Everything is meaningless."
What does man gain from all his labor at which he toils
under the sun? Generations come and generations go,
but the earth remains forever. The sun rises and
the sun sets, and hurries back to where it rises.

전도자가 말한다. 헛되고 헛되다. 헛되고 헛되다.
모든 것이 헛되다.
사람이 세상에서 아무리 수고한들, 무슨 보람이 있는가?
한 세대가 가고, 또 한 세대가 오지만, 세상은 언제나 그대로다.
해는 여전히 뜨고, 또 여전히 져서, 제자리로 돌아가며, 거기에서 다시 떠오른다. (전도서 1장)

"Meaningless! Meaningless!" says the Teacher.
"Utterly meaningless! Everything is meaningless."
What does man gain from all his labor at which he toils
under the sun? Generations come and generations go,
but the earth remains forever. The sun rises and
the sun sets, and hurries back to where it rises.

필기체 대문자와 소문자를 써보세요.

C C c

C

c

C c

속담과 격언속에서 만나는 단어

cast 던지다

cast cast

The die is cast.
주사위는 던져졌다.

The die is cast.

come 오다

come come

Death always comes too early or too late.
죽음은 늘 너무 빨리 찾아오든가 너무 늦게 찾아온다.

Death always comes too early or too late.

country 나라

country   country

A prophet has no honor in his own country.
선지자는 자기 조국에선 존경을 받지 못한다.

A prophet has no honor in his own country.

cross 십자가

cross   cross

No cross, no crown.
십자가 (고난) 없이는 왕관도 없다.

No cross, no crown.

cry 울다

cry   cry

Don't cry over spilt milk.
엎질러진 우유를 놓고 울지 말라.

Don't cry over spilt milk.

Courage is very important.
Like a muscle, it is strengthened by use.
용기는 대단히 중요하다. 근육과 같이, 사용함으로써 강해진다.

Courage is very important.

Like a muscle, it is strengthened by use.

Consider that men will do the same things
nevertheless, even though thou shouldst burst.
그대가 아무리 통탄할지라도, 사람들은 아랑곳하지 않고 같은 짓을 하리라.

Consider that men will do the same things

nevertheless, even though thou shouldst burst.

Common sense is the collection of prejudices
acquired by age 18.
상식은 18세 때까지 후천적으로 얻은 편견의 집합이다.

Common sense is the collection of prejudices

acquired by age 18.

● 나도 작가처럼

Two cheers for democracy:
one because it admits
variety and two because it permits criticism.
Two cheers are quite enough:
There is no occasion to give three.

민주주의에 대하여 박수를 보내는 이유는 두 가지이다.
첫째는 그것이 다양성을 인정하기 때문이고 둘째는 그것이 비판을 허용하기 때문이다.
이 두가지면 충분하다. 세번째 이유는 필요하지 않다.
(포스터)

Two cheers for democracy:

one because it admits

variety and two because it permits criticism.

Two cheers are quite enough:

There is no occasion to give three.

필기체 대문자와 소문자를 써보세요.

D *D d*

D

d

D d

속담과 격언속에서 만나는 단어

day 하루, 요일

day   day

What day is it today?
오늘 무슨 요일이지?

What day is it today?

dead 죽은

dead   dead

Dead men tell no tales.
죽은 사람은 말이 없다.

Dead men tell no tales.

diligence 근면

diligence   diligence

Diligence is the mother of good fortune.
근면은 행운의 어머니.

Diligence is the mother of good fortune.

dog 개

dog   dog

Dogs are more sociable than wolves.
개는 늑대보다 더 사회적이다.

Dogs are more sociable than wolves.

doubt 의심하다

doubt   doubt

To doubt is safer than to be secure.
의심하는 것이 확신하는 것보다 더 안전하다.

To doubt is safer than to be secure.

명언 여행

Death is the end of a lifetime.
Denial of death is a denial that time will end.
죽음은 삶의 끝이다. 죽음을 부정하는 것은 시간이 끝날 것이라는 사실을 부정하는 것이다.

Death is the end of a lifetime.

Denial of death is a denial that time will end.

Do not rejoice over anyone's death; remember that we all must die.
누군가의 죽음에 기뻐하지 말라. 우리 모두 반드시 죽는다는 걸 기억하라.

Do not rejoice over anyone's death; remember that

we all must die.

Discussion is an exchange of knowledge; argument an exchange of ignorance.
토론은 지식을 교환하는 것이고, 말싸움은 무지를 교환하는 것이다.

Discussion is an exchange of knowledge;

argument an exchange of ignorance.

● 나도 작가처럼

When love beckons to you, follow him,
Though his ways are hard and steep.
And when his wings enfold you yield to him,
Though the sword hidden among his pinions may
wound you.

사랑이 그대를 부르면 그를 따르라,
비록 그 길이 힘들고 가파를지라도.
사랑의 날개가 그대들을 감싸 안을 땐, 몸을 내맡기라
비록 사랑의 날개 속에 숨은 칼이 그대에게 상처를 입힐지라도.
(칼릴 지브란 '예언자' - 사랑에 대하여)

When love beckons to you, follow him,
Though his ways are hard and steep.
And when his wings enfold you yield to him,
Though the sword hidden among his pinions may
wound you.

◯ 필기체 대문자와 소문자를 써보세요.

E Ɛ e

E

e

E e

◯ 속담과 격언속에서 만나는 단어

eagle 독수리

eagle eagle

Eagles don't catch flies.
독수리는 파리를 잡지 않는다.

Eagles don't catch flies.

easy 쉬운

easy easy

Easy come, easy go.
쉽게 들어온 것은 쉽게 나간다.

Easy come, easy go.

E

empty 빈

empty empty

Empty wagons are the nosiest.
빈 마차가 가장 시끄럽다.

Empty wagons are the nosiest.

even ~조차도

even even

Even the greatest make mistakes.
대가도 실수할 수가 있다. (원숭이도 나무에서 떨어진다.)

Even the greatest make mistakes.

eye 눈

eye eye

An eye for an eye, and a tooth for a tooth.
눈에는 눈, 이에는 이.

An eye for an eye, and a tooth for a tooth.

◉ 명언 여행

Every generation laughs at the old fashions but religiously follows the new.
모든 세대는 지난 유행을 비웃지만, 새 유행도 어김없이 그 길을 따라간다.

Every generation laughs at the old fashions but

religiously follows the new.

Education has produced a vast population able to read but unable to distinguish what is worth reading.
교육은 수많은 사람에게 글씨는 가르쳤지만 읽을 가치가 있는 것을 구별하는 능력은 길러주지 못했다.

Education has produced a vast population able to read

but unable to distinguish what is worth reading.

Everyone thinks of changing the world, but no one thinks of changing himself.
누구나 세상을 바꾸는 것에 대해 생각하지만, 누구도 자신을 바꾸는 것에 대해서는 생각하지 않는다.

Everyone thinks of changing the world, but no one

thinks of changing himself.

🔴 나도 작가처럼

From my grandfather Verus I learned good morals
and the government of my temper.
From the reputation and remembrance of my father,
modesty and a manly character.

할아버지 베루스에게서 나는 훌륭한 품행을
그리고 노여움을 다스리는 법을 배웠다.
아버지에 대한 명성과 추억으로부터 나는
겸손과 남자다운 기상을 배웠다.
(아우렐리우스 '명상록')

From my grandfather Verus I learned good morals
and the government of my temper.
From the reputation and remembrance of my father,
modesty and a manly character.

✏️ 필기체 대문자와 소문자를 써보세요.

F f

● 속담과 격언속에서 만나는 단어

faint 소심한

faint faint

Faint heart never won fair lady.

겁쟁이는 미인을 차지할 수 없다.

Faint heart never won fair lady.

faith 믿음

faith faith

Faith can remove mountains.

믿음은 산도 옮길 수 있다.

Faith can remove mountains.

fish 물고기

fish fish

A big fish must swim in deep waters.
큰 물고기는 큰물에서 놀아야 한다.

A big fish must swim in deep waters.

flow 흐름, 유입

flow flow

Every flow must have its ebb.
밀물이 있으면 썰물이 있다.

Every flow must have its ebb.

friend 친구

friend friend

A friend in need is a friend indeed.
곤경에 빠졌을 때의 친구가 참다운 친구이다.

A friend in need is a friend indeed.

Freedom is not procured by a full enjoy of what is desired, but by controlling the desire.

자유는 원하는 걸 온전히 즐김으로써 얻어지는 게 아니라, 욕망을 억제함으로써 얻어지는 것이다.

Freedom is not procured by a full enjoy of what is desired, but by controlling the desire.

Who controls the past controls the future.
Who controls the present controls the past.

과거를 지배하는 자는 미래를 지배한다. 현재를 지배하는 자는 과거를 지배한다.

Who controls the past controls the future.
Who controls the present controls the past.

First you take a drink, then the drink takes a drink, then the drink takes you.

처음에는 당신이 술을 마시고, 다음에는 술이 술을 마시고, 다음에는 술이 당신을 마신다.

First you take a drink, then the drink takes a drink, then the drink takes you.

● 나도 작가처럼

The mystery of language was revealed to me.
I knew then that "w-a-t-e-r" meant the wonderful
cool something that was flowing over my hand.
That living word awakened my soul, gave it light,
joy, set it free!

언어의 신비가 나에게 나타났다.
그때 나는 "w-a-t-e-r"가 내 손위로 흐르는 멋지고 시원한 그 어떤 것임을 알았다.
그같이 살아 있는 말이 내 영혼을 일깨우고 빛과 기쁨을 주고 자유롭게 만들어 주었다.
(헬렌 켈러)

The mystery of language was revealed to me.
I knew then that "w-a-t-e-r" meant the wonderful
cool something that was flowing over my hand.
That living word awakened my soul, gave it light,
joy, set it free!

필기체 대문자와 소문자를 써보세요.

G $\mathcal{G}$ g

속담과 격언속에서 만나는 단어

glitter 반짝이다

glitter   glitter

All that glitters is not gold.
반짝인다고 다 금은 아니다.

All that glitters is not gold.

glory 영광, 영예

glory   glory

Glory is the fair child of peril.
호랑이 굴에 들어가야 호랑이를 잡는다.

Glory is the fair child of peril.

gold 금

gold gold

Fire is the test of gold; adversity, of strong men.
불은 황금을 시험하고, 역경은 강한 사람들을 시험한다.

Fire is the test of gold; adversity, of strong men.

good 좋은

good good

A good medicine tastes bitter.
좋은 약은 맛이 쓰다.

A good medicine tastes bitter.

grave 무덤

grave grave

From the cradle to the grave.
요람에서 무덤까지.

From the cradle to the grave.

◉ 명언 여행

A man of genius makes no mistakes.
His errors are volitional and are portals of discovery.
천재는 실수하지 않는다. 그의 실수는 의지에서 나온 것이고 발견의 통로가 된다.

A man of genius makes no mistakes.

His errors are volitional and are portals of discovery.

Our greatest glory consists not in never falling but in rising every time we fall.
우리의 가장 큰 영광은 한번도 실패를 안 하는 것에 있는 것이 아니라, 실패할 때마다 일어서는데 있다.

Our greatest glory consists not in never falling but in

rising every time we fall.

Genius is one percent inspiration and ninety-nine percent perspiration.
천재는 1퍼센트의 영감과 99퍼센트의 땀으로 이루어진다.

Genius is one percent inspiration and ninety-nine

percent perspiration.

◉ 나도 작가처럼

> We are an intelligent species and the use of our intelligence quite properly gives us pleasure.
> In this respect the brain is like a muscle.
> When it is in use we feel very good.
> Understanding is joyous.
>
> 우리는 지성적 존재이므로 당연히 지성을 사용할 때 기쁨을 느낀다.
> 이런 의미에서 두뇌는 근육과 같다.
> 두뇌를 사용할 때 우리는 기분이 매우 좋아진다.
> 이해한다는 것은 즐거운 일이다.
> (칼 세이건)

We are an intelligent species and the use of our

intelligence quite properly gives us pleasure.

In this respect the brain is like a muscle.

When it is in use we feel very good.

Understanding is joyous.

필기체 대문자와 소문자를 써보세요.

H

H *h*

H h

속담과 격언속에서 만나는 단어

health 건강

health health

Good health is a great asset.
건강이 큰 재산이다.

Good health is a great asset.

help 돕다

help help

God helps the early riser.
하늘은 일찍 일어나는 사람을 돕는다.

God helps the early riser.

history 역사

history history

History repeats itself.
역사는 되풀이 된다.

History repeats itself.

honesty 정직

honesty honesty

Honesty is the best policy.
정직이 최상의 방책이다.

Honesty is the best policy.

hungry 배고픈

hungry hungry

A hungry ass eats any straw.
배고픈 당나귀는 짚을 가리지 않는다. (시장이 반찬이다.)

A hungry ass eats any straw.

명언 여행

The health produces the pleasure, the pleasure produces the wealth.

건강은 즐거움을 낳고, 즐거움은 부를 낳는다.

The health produces the pleasure, the pleasure produces the wealth.

If you want to be happy for a year, plant a garden; if you want to be happy for life, plant a tree.

1년간의 행복을 위해서는 정원을 가꾸고, 평생의 행복을 원한다면 나무를 심어라.

If you want to be happy for a year, plant a garden; if you want to be happy for life, plant a tree.

You may lead a horse to the water, but you cannot make him drink.

말을 물가에 데리고 갈 수는 있어도 물을 먹일 수는 없다.

You may lead a horse to the water, but you cannot make him drink.

나도 작가처럼

It took me a long time to learn where he came from.
The little prince, who asked me so many questions,
never seemed to hear the ones I asked him.
It was from words dropped by chance that,
little by little, everything was revealed to me.

그가 어디서 왔는지를 아는 데는 오랜 시일이 걸렸다.
어린 왕자는 내게 많은 것을 물어보면서도 내 질문에는 귀를 기울이는 것 같지 않았다.
그가 우연히 뱉은 말들이 차츰차츰 모든 것을 알게 해주었다.
(생텍쥐페리 '어린 왕자')

It took me a long time to learn where he came from.
The little prince, who asked me so many questions,
never seemed to hear the ones I asked him.
It was from words dropped by chance that,
little by little, everything was revealed to me.

필기체 대문자와 소문자를 써보세요.

I l i

I

i

$I \; i$

속담과 격언속에서 만나는 단어

if 만약~라면

if if

If you want peace, prepare for war.
평화를 원한다면, 전쟁 준비를 해라.

If you want peace, prepare for war.

ignorance 무지

ignorance ignorance

Ignorance is bliss.
무지는 축복이다. (모르는 게 약.)

Ignorance is bliss.

industry 근면

industry industry

Industry is the parent of success.
근면은 성공의 부모이다.

Industry is the parent of success.

interest 관심사

interest interest

His main interests are music and tennis.
그의 주된 관심사는 음악과 테니스이다.

His main interests are music and tennis.

invalid 환자

invalid invalid

Every invalid is a physician.
환자는 전부 의사이다.

Every invalid is a physician.

Intelligence recognizes what has happened.
Genius recognizes what will happen.
지적인 사람은 일어난 일을 안다. 천재는 일어날 일을 안다.

Intelligence recognizes what has happened.

Genius recognizes what will happen.

Life is the art of drawing sufficient conclusions
from insufficient premises.
인생이란 불만족스러운 전제로부터 만족스러운 결론을 끌어내는 기술이다.

Life is the art of drawing sufficient conclusions

from insufficient premises.

In giving advice, seek to help, not to please,
your friend.
충고할 때 친구를 만족시키려 하지 말고, 친구에게 도움이 되도록 하라.

In giving advice, seek to help, not to please,

your friend.

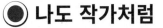

나도 작가처럼

Yet he dismisses without notice his thought, because it is his. In every work of genius we recognize our own rejected thoughts; they come back to us with a certain alienated majesty.

그러나 인간은 자기에서 나왔다는 이유로 자기의 생각을 묵살합니다.
모든 천재들의 작품 속에서 우리는 우리가 거절했던 사상들을 발견합니다. 우리가 묵살했던 사상들이
이제는 우리가 도달할 수 없는 위엄을 가지고 우리에게 되돌아옵니다.
(에머슨 '자립 Self-reliance')

Yet he dismisses without notice his thought,
because it is his. In every work of genius we recognize
our own rejected thoughts; they come back to us with
a certain alienated majesty.

필기체 대문자와 소문자를 써보세요.

J $\mathscr{J}$ j

$\mathscr{J}$

j

$\mathscr{J}$ j

속담과 격언속에서 만나는 단어

Jack of all trades
무엇이든 잘 할 수 있는 사람

Jack of all trades   *Jack of all trades*

Jack of all trades is master of none.
많은 것을 잘하면 특별히 잘 하는게 없다.

Jack of all trades is master of none.

join 합류하다

join   join

Will you join us for lunch?
우리와 함께 점심 할래요?

Will you join us for lunch?

journey 여행

journey journey

Life is a long journey.
인생은 긴 여행이다.

Life is a long journey.

joy 기쁨

joy joy

One joy scatters a hundred griefs.
한 가지 기쁨이 백 가지 슬픔을 쫓아낸다.

One joy scatters a hundred griefs.

judge 판단하다

judge judge

Don't judge of a man by his looks.
사람을 외모로 판단하지 말라.

Don't judge of a man by his looks.

명언 여행

Love is not simply giving; it is judicious giving and judicious withholding as well.

사랑은 단순히 주는 것이 아니라, 사려 깊게 주고 또한 사려 깊게 물러서는 것이다.

Love is not simply giving; it is judicious giving and judicious withholding as well.

The object of studying philosophy is to know one's own mind, not other people's.

철학을 공부하는 목적은 다른 사람들의 마음이 아니라, 자신의 마음을 알려는 데 있다.

The object of studying philosophy is to know one's own mind, not other people's.

If you do not walk today, you will have to run tomorrow.

오늘 걷지 않으면, 내일은 뛰어야 한다.

If you do not walk today, you will have to run tomorrow.

● 나도 작가처럼

A throng of bearded men, in sad-coloured garments and grey steeple-crowned hats, inter-mixed with women, some wearing hoods, and others bareheaded, was assembled in front of a wooden edifice, the door of which was heavily timbered with oak, and studded with iron spikes.

우중충한 회색 옷차림에 고깔모자를 쓰고 수염이 텁수룩한 남자들이 더러는 수건을 쓰고 더러는 쓰지 않은 여인들과 함께한 목조 건물 앞에 서 있었다. 그 건물의 대문은 육중한 참나무이고 표면에는 뾰족하고 큰 쇠못이 촘촘히 박혀 있었다.
(나다니엘 호손 '주홍글씨' - 첫 문장, 문예출판사)

필기체 대문자와 소문자를 써보세요.

K K k

K

k

K k

속담과 격언속에서 만나는 단어

keep 유지하다, 계속하다

keep keep

When money speaks, the truth keeps silent.
돈이 말할 때, 진실은 침묵한다.

When money speaks, the truth keeps silent.

kill 죽이다

kill kill

To kill two birds with one stone.
돌멩이 하나로 새 두 마리 잡기. (일석이조. 一石二鳥)

To kill two birds with one stone.

kind 종류

kind kind

What kind of music do you like?
어떤 종류의 음악을 좋아하세요?

What kind of music do you like?

know 알다

know know

To know is one thing, to teach is another.
아는 것과 가르치는 것은 별개다.

To know is one thing, to teach is another.

knowledge 지식

knowledge knowledge

Knowledge in youth is wisdom in age.
젊어서 얻은 지식은 늙어서 지혜가 된다.

Knowledge in youth is wisdom in age.

◉ 명언 여행

Knowledge of human nature is the beginning and end of political education.
인간 본성에 대한 지식이 정치 교육의 시작이자 끝이다.

Knowledge of human nature is the beginning and end of political education.

The best and most beautiful things in the world cannot be seen of even touched. They must be felt with the heart.
세상에서 가장 아름답고 소중한 것은 보이거나 만져지지 않는다. 단지 가슴으로만 느낄 수 있다.

The best and most beautiful things in the world cannot be seen of even touched. They must be felt with the heart.

The world is a beautiful book, but of little use to him who cannot read it.
세상은 한 권의 아름다운 책이지만 그 책을 읽을 수 없는 사람에게는 별 소용이 없다.

The world is a beautiful book, but of little use to him who cannot read it.

◉ 나도 작가처럼

Call me Ishmael. Some years ago-never mind how long precisely-having little or no money in my purse, and nothing particular to interest me on shore, I thought I would sail about a little and see the watery part of the world.

내 이름을 이슈메일이라고 해두자. 몇 년 전-정확히 언제인지는 아무래도 좋다
-지갑은 거의 바닥이 났고 또 뭍에는 딱히 흥미를 끄는 것이 없었으므로,
당분간 배를 타고 나가서 세계의 바다를 두루 돌아보면 좋겠다는 생각을 했다.
(허먼 멜빌 '모비딕' - 첫 문장. 김석희 역)

Call me Ishmael. Some years ago-never mind how long precisely-having little or no money in my purse, and nothing particular to interest me on shore, I thought I would sail about a little and see the watery part of the world.

L *L* *l*

L

l

L l

leak 새는 곳

leak leak

A small leak will sink a great ship.
작은 구멍이 거대한 배도 가라앉힌다.

A small leak will sink a great ship.

leave 떠나다

leave leave

Leave a welcome behind you.
환영받을 때 떠나라.

Leave a welcome behind you.

life 인생

life   life

Life is full of ups and downs.
인생은 오르막길과 내리막길로 꽉 차 있다.

Life is full of ups and downs.

love 사랑

love   love

Love thy neighbor as thyself.
네 이웃을 네 몸처럼 사랑하라.

Love thy neighbor as thyself.

luck 행운

luck   luck

Good luck does not always repeat itself.
행운은 늘 되풀이해서 일어나진 않는다.

Good luck does not always repeat itself.

◉ 명언 여행

Like all great travelers, I have seen more than I remember, and remember more than I have seen.
훌륭한 여행가들이 흔히 그렇듯이 나는 내가 기억하는 것보다 많은 것을 보았고 또한 본 것보다 많은 것을 기억한다.

Like all great travelers, I have seen more than I

remember, and remember more than I have seen.

Life improves slowly and goes wrong fast, and only catastrophe is clearly visible.
삶은 천천히 나아지고 빨리 나빠지며, 큰 재난만 선명하게 눈에 보일 뿐이다.

Life improves slowly and goes wrong fast,

and only catastrophe is clearly visible.

Liberty without learning is always in peril and learning without liberty is always in vain.
배움이 없는 자유는 언제나 위험하며 자유가 없는 배움은 언제나 헛된 것이다.

Liberty without learning is always in peril and

learning without liberty is always in vain.

● 나도 작가처럼

To be, or not to be, that is the question,
Whether 'tis nobler in the mind to suffer.
The slings and arrows of outrageous fortune,
Or to take arms against a sea of troubles,
And by opposing end them? To die; to sleep;

살아 부지할 것인가, 죽어 없어질 것인가, 그것이 문제다.
가혹한 운명의 돌팔매와 화살을 받고,
참는 것이 장한 정신이냐? 아니면 조수처럼 밀려드는 환난을 두 손으로 막아,
그를 없이 함이 장한 정신이냐? 죽는 일은 자는 일. 다만 그뿐이다.
(셰익스피어 '햄릿' - 3막, 올재클래식)

To be, or not to be, that is the question,

Whether 'tis nobler in the mind to suffer.

The slings and arrows of outrageous fortune,

Or to take arms against a sea of troubles,

And by opposing end them? To die; to sleep;

필기체 대문자와 소문자를 써보세요.

$\mathcal{M}$ $\mathcal{m}$ $\mathcal{m}$

$\mathcal{M}$

$\mathcal{m}$

$\mathcal{M}$ $\mathcal{m}$

속담과 격언속에서 만나는 단어

magic 마술, 신비

magic   magic

The magic of first love is our ignorance that it can ever end.
첫사랑이 신비로운 것은 그것이 언젠가는 끝날 수 있다는 것을 우리가 알지 못하기 때문이다.

The magic of first love is our ignorance that it can ever end.

make 만들다, ~하게 하다

make   make

Many drops make a shower.
많은 물방울이 소나기가 된다. (티끌 모아 태산.)

Many drops make a shower.

060

man 인간

man   man

Man, know thyself. All wisdom centers there.
인간이여, 네 자신을 알라. 모든 지혜는 거기 몰려 있다.

Man, know thyself. All wisdom centers there.

misfortune 불행

misfortune   misfortune

Misfortunes never come single.
불행은 절대 혼자 오지 않는다.

Misfortunes never come single.

money 돈

money   money

Money begets money.
돈이 돈을 번다.

Money begets money.

**Friendship is the marriage of the soul,
and this marriage is liable to divorce.**

우정은 영혼의 결혼이다. 그리고 이 결혼은 깨지기 쉽다.

Friendship is the marriage of the soul,

and this marriage is liable to divorce.

**It is only with the heart that one can see rightly;
what is essential is invisible to the eye.**

사람은 오로지 가슴으로만 올바로 볼 수 있다. 본질적인 것은 눈에 보이지 않기 때문이다.

It is only with the heart that one can see rightly;

what is essential is invisible to the eye.

**We hold these truths to be self-evident,
that all men and women are created equal.**

우리는 모든 남자와 여자가 평등하게 태어났다는 것을 자명한 진실로 생각한다.

We hold these truths to be self-evident,

that all men and women are created equal.

● 나도 작가처럼

Maman died today. Or yesterday maybe, I don't know.
I got a telegram from the home;
"Mother deceased. Funeral tomorrow. Faithfully yours."
That doesn't mean anything.
Maybe it was yesterday.

오늘 엄마가 돌아가셨다. 아니 어쩌면 어제인지도 모르겠다.
양로원에서 전보를 보내왔다.
'모친 사망. 내일 장례식. 근조.' 그것으로는 알 수가 없다.
어쩌면 어제였을지도 모른다.
(알베르 카뮈 '이방인' - 첫 문장)

Maman died today. Or yesterday maybe, I don't know.
I got a telegram from the home;
"Mother deceased. Funeral tomorrow. Faithfully yours."
That doesn't mean anything.
Maybe it was yesterday.

필기체 대문자와 소문자를 써보세요.

N *N* *n*

N

n

N n

속담과 격언속에서 만나는 단어

nature 자연

nature   nature

Nature abhors a vacuum.
자연은 진공을 싫어한다.

Nature abhors a vacuum.

near 가까운

near   near

Near neighbor is better than a distant cousin.
가까운 이웃이 먼 사촌보다 낫다. (이웃사촌.)

Near neighbor is better than a distant cousin.

necessity 필요

necessity   necessity

Necessity is the mother of invention.
필요는 발명의 어머니.

Necessity is the mother of invention.

news 뉴스

news   news

No news is good news.
무소식이 희소식.

No news is good news.

nothing 아무것도 ~아니다

nothing   nothing

Nothing can be accomplished without effort.
노력 없이 이루어지는 일은 없다.

Nothing can be accomplished without effort.

Nature never deceives us; it is always we who deceive ourselves.

자연은 인간을 결코 속이지 않는다. 우리를 속이는 것은 항상 우리 자신이다.

Nature never deceives us; it is always we who deceive ourselves.

No human being can really understand another, and no one can arrange another's happiness.

그 누구도 다른 사람을 정말로 이해할 수 없고, 그 누구도 다른 사람의 행복을 만들어 줄 수 없다.

No human being can really understand another, and no one can arrange another's happiness.

This is my simple religion. There is no need for temples; no need for complicated philosophy.

이것이 나의 단순한 종교다. 이 종교에는 사원도, 복잡한 철학도 필요 없다.

This is my simple religion. There is no need for temples; no need for complicated philosophy.

● 나도 작가처럼

I have no understanding of it and I am not sure that I believe in it. Perhaps it was a sin to kill the fish. I suppose it was even though I did it to keep me alive and feed many people.
But then everything is a sin.

나는 죄가 뭔지 모르겠고 또 그런 게 있다고 믿고 있는지도 확실하지 않아.
그렇더라도 아마 그 고기를 죽인 것은 죄가 될 거야. 내가 살기 위해서,
또 여러 사람에게 먹이기 위해서 그렇게 했다 할지라도 그것은 죄야.
하지만 그렇다면 무엇이든 죄가 아닌 게 없을 테지.
(헤밍웨이 '노인과 바다')

I have no understanding of it and I am not sure that
I believe in it. Perhaps it was a sin to kill the fish.
I suppose it was even though I did it to keep me alive
and feed many people.
But then everything is a sin.

필기체 대문자와 소문자를 써보세요.

$\mathcal{O}$

$\mathcal{O}$ $\mathcal{o}$

속담과 격언속에서 만나는 단어

offer 제공하다

offer offer

What can I offer you to drink?
마실 것 좀 가져다드릴까요?

What can I offer you to drink?

old 오래된

old old

Old friends and old wine are best.
친구와 포도주는 오래된 것이 좋다.

Old friends and old wine are best.

one 하나

one one

One generation plants the trees; another gets the shade.
한 세대가 나무를 심고 다른 세대가 그 그늘을 취한다.

One generation plants the trees; another gets the shade.

only 오로지

only only

Only the just man enjoys peace of mind.
정의로운 사람만이 마음의 평화를 누린다.

Only the just man enjoys peace of mind.

out of 없는, 벗어나서

out of out of

Out of sight, out of mind.
보지 않으면 마음도 멀어진다.

Out of sight, out of mind.

◉ 명언 여행

One of the chief causes of lack of zest is the feeling that one is unloved.
열정이 부족해지는 주된 이유들 중 하나는 자신이 사랑받지 못하고 있다는 느낌이다.

One of the chief causes of lack of zest is the feeling

that one is unloved.

Often think of the rapidity with which things pass by and disappear, both the things which are and the things which are produced.
스스로 존재하는 사물들과 만들어져서 존재하는 것들이 얼마나 빨리 흘러가고 사라지는지를 자주 생각하라.

Often think of the rapidity with which things pass by and disappear,

both the things which are and the things which are produced.

Love does not consist in gazing at each other, but in looking together in the same direction.
사랑은 두 사람이 마주보는 것이 아니라, 함께 같은 방향을 바라보는 것이다.

Love does not consist in gazing at each other,

but in looking together in the same direction.

● 나도 작가처럼

From my mother, I learned piety and beneficence,
and abstinence, not only from evil deeds,
but even from evil thoughts;
and further, simplicity in my way of living,
far removed from the habits of the rich.

어머니에게서 나는 사악한 행위들뿐 아니라 사악한 생각까지도 삼가는 절제와,
경건한 마음과 너그러움을 배웠으며, 나아가서 살아가는 방법에 있어서는 부유한 사람들의
습성을 멀리 피하여 검소하게 살아가라는 가르침을 받았다.
(아우렐리우스 '명상록')

From my mother, I learned piety and beneficence,
and abstinence, not only from evil deeds,
but even from evil thoughts;
and further, simplicity in my way of living,
far removed from the habits of the rich.

필기체 대문자와 소문자를 써보세요.

P   𝒫   𝓅

𝒫

𝓅

𝒫 𝓅

속담과 격언속에서 만나는 단어

pain 고통

pain   pain

No pains, no gains.
수고 없이는 소득도 없다.

No pains, no gains.

pearl 진주

pearl   pearl

Do not cast pearls before swine.
돼지 앞에 진주를 던지지 말라.

Do not cast pearls before swine.

pie 파이

pie pie

Pie in the sky.
하늘에 있는 파이. (그림의 떡.)

Pie in the sky.

poet 시인

poet poet

A poet is the painter of the soul.
시인은 영혼의 화가이다.

A poet is the painter of the soul.

petty 사소한

petty petty

Petty crimes are punished: great, rewarded.
작은 죄는 벌을 받고, 큰 죄는 상을 받는다.

Petty crimes are punished: great, rewarded.

명언 여행

Since a politician never believes what he says, he is surprised when others believe him.
정치가는 자신이 한 말을 믿지 않기 때문에, 다른 사람들이 자신을 믿으면 놀랜다.

Since a politician never believes what he says,

he is surprised when others believe him.

It's not just enough to change the players. We've gotta change the game.
선수(정치인)들을 교체하는 것만으로는 충분하지 않다. 그 게임(정치)을 바꾸어야 한다.

It's not just enough to change the players.

We've gotta change the game.

The person with a passion for what he or she does become a peak performer.
자기가 하는 일에 열정을 가진 사람은 최고의 성취를 이루는 사람이 된다.

The person with a passion for what he or she does

become a peak performer.

● 나도 작가처럼

If you really want to hear about it, the first thing you'll probably want to know is where I was born, and what my lousy childhood was like, and how my parents were occupied and all before they had me, and all that David Copperfield kind of crap, but I don't feel like going into it, if you want to know the truth.

네가 정말로 이 이야기에 대해 듣고 싶다면, 우선 내가 어디서 태어났는지, 내 어린 시절이 얼마나 끔찍했는지, 내 부모님은 무슨 직업을 가지고 있었는지, 내가 태어나기 전엔 어떤 일이 있었는지 같은 데이비드 코퍼필드 식의 쓸데없는 이야기에 대해서 듣고 싶을 것이다. 하지만 난 그런 이야기는 하고 싶지 않다.
(샐린저 '호밀밭의 파수꾼' - 첫 문장)

If you really want to hear about it, the first thing you'll
probably want to know is where I was born, and what
my lousy childhood was like, and how my parents were
occupied and all before they had me, and all that David
Copperfield kind of crap, but I don't feel like going into it,
if you want to know the truth.

필기체 대문자와 소문자를 써보세요.

Q Q q

Q

q

Q q

속담과 격언속에서 만나는 단어

queen 여왕

queen queen

The rose is the queen of flowers.
장미는 꽃의 여왕이다.

The rose is the queen of flowers.

question 질문

question question

Question is not answer.
질문은 답이 아니다.

Question is not answer.

quick 빠른

quick   quick

Be slow to promise, quick to perform.
약속은 천천히 하고, 실행은 빨리하라.

Be slow to promise, quick to perform.

quit 그만두다

quit   quit

I've quit smoking.
난 담배 끊었어.

I've quit smoking.

quite 꽤, 더없이

quite   quite

Business? It's quite simple. It's other people's money.
사업? 그건 아주 간단하다. 다른 사람들의 돈이다.

Business? It's quite simple. It's other people's money.

명언 여행

The quality of the relationship between you and your self is paramount, for all your other relationships are based on it.

당신과 당신 자아 사이에 이루어지는 관계의 속성이 가장 중요하다. 왜냐하면 당신의 다른 모든 관계들이 그것에 기초를 두고 있기 때문이다.

The quality of the relationship between you and your self is paramount, for all your other relationships are based on it.

A leader who loves the status quo soon becomes a follower.

현재의 상태에 안주하려는 지도자는 조만간 뒤쳐진 사람이 된다.

A leader who loves the status quo soon becomes a follower.

Practice the getting of tranquility by passing peaceful words and thoughts through your mind daily and nightly.

매일 밤낮으로 평화로운 말과 생각들이 당신의 마음을 통과하게 함으로써 고요를 얻는 연습을 하라.

Practice the getting of tranquility by passing peaceful words and thoughts through your mind daily and nightly.

● 나도 작가처럼

Those who are accustomed to judge by feeling do not understand
the process of reasoning, for they would understand at first
sight, and are not used to seek for principles. And others,
on the contrary, who are accustomed to reason from principles,
do not at all understand matters of feeling, seeking principles,
and being unable to see at a glance.

직감에 의해 판단하는 데 익숙한 사람들은 추리의 과정에 대해서는 조금도 이해하지 못한다.
그들은 한눈에 밑바닥까지 보려 하므로 원리를 찾는 일에 익숙하지 못하기 때문이다.
이와 반대로 원리를 바탕 삼아 추리하는 데 익숙한 사람들은 직감해야 할 사항을 조금도 이해하지 못한다.
그들은 원리를 찾느라고 사물을 한눈에 통찰할 수 없기 때문이다. (파스칼 '팡세')

Those who are accustomed to judge by feeling do not understand
the process of reasoning, for they would understand at first
sight, and are not used to seek for principles. And others,
on the contrary, who are accustomed to reason from principles,
do not at all understand matters of feeling, seeking principles,
and being unable to see at a glance.

필기체 대문자와 소문자를 써보세요.

R   R   r

R

r

R r

속담과 격언속에서 만나는 단어

repentance 후회

repentance   repentance

Repentance comes too late.
후회는 너무 늦게 온다.

Repentance comes too late.

road 길

road   road

All roads lead to Rome.
모든 길은 로마로 통한다.

All roads lead to Rome.

rolling 구르는

rolling rolling

A rolling stone gathers no moss.
구르는 돌에는 이끼가 끼지 않다.

A rolling stone gathers no moss.

Rome 로마

Rome Rome

Do in Rome as the Romans do.
로마에선 로마인들이 하는 대로 해라.

Do in Rome as the Romans do.

royal 국왕의

royal royal

There is no royal road to learning.
배움에는 왕도가 없다.

There is no royal road to learning.

Everyone has been created to have relationships, first with God and then with others.

누구나 관계를 가지도록 창조되었으며, 먼저 신과 관계를 맺은 후 다음으로 다른 사람들과 관계를 맺게 되어있다.

Everyone has been created to have relationships,

first with God and then with others.

The winds and waves are always on the side of the ablest navigators.

바람과 파도는 항상 가장 유능한 항해자의 편에 선다.

The winds and waves are always on the side of the

ablest navigators.

The higher the level of consciousness, the greater the likelyhood that what is held in mind will actualize.

의식의 수준이 높을수록 마음 속에 있는 것이 실현될 수 있는 가능성이 커진다.

The higher the level of consciousness, the greater the

likelyhood that what is held in mind will actualize.

● 나도 작가처럼

I believe there are more instances of the abridgment of the freedom of the people by gradual and silent encroachments of those in power than by violent and sudden usurpations.

폭력적이고 갑작스러운 강탈행위에 의해서 보다는 권력을 쥐고 있는 이들의 점진적이고도 소리 없는 침입에 의해 사람들의 자유가 축소되는 사례가 더 많다고 나는 믿고 있다.
(제임스 매디슨)

I believe there are more instances of the abridgment
of the freedom of the people by gradual and silent
encroachments of those in power than by violent and
sudden usurpations.

필기체 대문자와 소문자를 써보세요.

S

속담과 격언속에서 만나는 단어

see 보다

see see

Seeing is believing.
보는 것이 믿는 것이다.

Seeing is believing.

smoke 연기

smoke smoke

No smoke without fire.
불 없이는 연기가 날 수 없다.

No smoke without fire.

soldier 병사

soldier   soldier

Old soldiers never die; They just fade away.
노병은 죽지 않는다. 다만 사라질 뿐이다.

Old soldiers never die; They just fade away.

sound 건전한

sound   sound

A sound mind in a sound body.
건전한 신체에 건전한 정신.

A sound mind in a sound body.

strike 때리다

strike   strike

Strike while the iron is hot.
쇠가 달았을 때 때려라. (쇠뿔도 단김에 빼라.)

Strike while the iron is hot.

● 명언 여행

A sudden, bold, and unexpected question doth many times surprise a man and lay him open.
예상 밖의 갑작스럽고 대담한 질문은 한 인간을 여러 번 놀라게 해서 그의 정체를 드러나게 한다.

A sudden, bold, and unexpected question doth many times surprise a man and lay him open.

The secret of business is to know something that nobody else knows.
사업의 비결은 다른 사람들은 모르고 있는 무엇인가를 아는 것이다.

The secret of business is to know something that nobody else knows.

If a man takes no thought about what is distant, he will find sorrow near at hand.
사람이 멀리 있는 일을 생각하지 않으면 바로 앞에 슬픔이 닥치는 법이다.

If a man takes no thought about what is distant, he will find sorrow near at hand.

나도 작가처럼

Do not think about sin. It is much too late
for that and there are people who are paid to do it.
Let them think about it. You were born to be a
fisherman as the fish was born to be a fish.

아무튼 지금은 죄를 생각하지 말자. 이제 와서 그런 생각을 하기에는 이미 늦었어.
그리고 돈을 받고 죄에 대해 생각해주는 사람들도 있으니까.
그런 사람들이나 죄에 대해 실컷 생각하라지.
물고기가 물고기로 태어난 것처럼 나는 어부가 되려고 태어난 거야.
(헤밍웨이 '노인과 바다')

Do not think about sin. It is much too late

for that and there are people who are paid to do it.

Let them think about it. You were born to be a

fisherman as the fish was born to be a fish.

필기체 대문자와 소문자를 써보세요.

$\mathcal{T}$ $\mathcal{T}$ t

$\mathcal{T}$ t

속담과 격언속에서 만나는 단어

think 생각하다

think think

I think, therefore I am.
나는 생각한다. 고로 존재한다.

I think, therefore I am.

thread 실

thread thread

To go together like needle and thread.
바늘 가는데 실 간다.

To go together like needle and thread.

today 오늘

today today

Think today and speak tomorrow.
오늘 생각하고 내일 말하라.

Think today and speak tomorrow.

travel 여행하다, 전해지다

travel travel

Bad news travels quickly.
나쁜 소문은 빨리 퍼진다.

Bad news travels quickly.

tree 나무

tree tree

The tree is known by its fruit.
나무는 그 열매로 알 수 있다.

The tree is known by its fruit.

명언 여행

There are two ways of spreading light; to be the candle or the mirror that reflects it.
빛을 퍼뜨릴 수 있는 두 가지 방법이 있다. 촛불이 되거나 또는 그것을 비추는 거울이 되는 것이다.

> *There are two ways of spreading light;*
> *to be the candle or the mirror that reflects it.*

Life is very short. And there's no time for fussing and fighting, my friends.
인생은 아주 짧아. 싸우거나 말다툼할 시간이 없다네, 친구여.

> *Life is very short. And there's no time for fussing and*
> *fighting, my friends.*

Although the world is full of suffering, it is full also of the overcoming of it.
세상은 고통으로 꽉 차 있지만, 한편으로 그것을 이겨내는 일로도 충만하다.

> *Although the world is full of suffering, it is full also*
> *of the overcoming of it.*

● 나도 작가처럼

Listen, my sons, to a father's instruction;
pay attention and gain understanding.
I give you sound learning, so do not forsake
my teaching.
When I was a boy in my father's house, still tender,
and an only child of my mother.

아이들아, 너희는 아버지의 훈계를 잘 듣고, 명철을 얻도록 귀를 기울여라.
내가 선한 도리를 너희에게 전하니,
너희는 내 교훈을 저버리지 말아라.
나도 내 아버지에게는 아들이었고,
내 어머니 앞에서도 하나뿐인 귀여운 자식이었다. (잠언 4장)

Listen, my sons, to a father's instruction;
pay attention and gain understanding.
I give you sound learning, so do not forsake
my teaching.
When I was a boy in my father's house, still tender,
and an only child of my mother.

필기체 대문자와 소문자를 써보세요.

U U u

U u

속담과 격언속에서 만나는 단어

under ~아래

under under

There is no new thing under the sun.
태양 아래 새로운 것은 아무것도 없다.

There is no new thing under the sun.

understand 이해하다

understand understand

No human being can really understand another.
그 누구도 다른 사람을 정말로 이해할 수는 없다.

No human being can really understand another.

united 단결된, 통일된

united united

United we stand, divided we fall.
뭉치면 살고, 흩어지면 죽는다.

United we stand, divided we fall.

unless ~하지 않는다면

unless unless

Unless you enter the tiger's den you cannot take the cubs.
호랑이 굴에 들어가야 호랑이 새끼를 잡을 수 있다.

Unless you enter the tiger's den you cannot take the cubs.

use 유용함

use use

It is no use crying over spilt milk.
엎질러진 우유를 놓고 울어봐야 소용없다.

It is no use crying over spilt milk.

> **The idea of parallel universe was first conceived by Hugh Everett III in 1957.**
> 평행우주라는 개념은 1957년 휴 에버렛 3세에 의해서 처음으로 생겨났다.

The idea of parallel universe was first conceived by Hugh Everett III in 1957.

> **He was an old man who fished alone in a skiff in the Gulf Stream and he had gone eighty-four days now without taking a fish.**
> 그는 멕시코 만류에 조각배를 띄우고 혼자 고기를 잡는 노인이었는데, 팔십사일이 되도록 물고기 한 마리도 잡지 못하고 있었다.

He was an old man who fished alone in a skiff in the Gulf Stream and he had gone eighty-four days now without taking a fish.

> **From fortune to misfortune is but a step; from misfortune to fortunes a long way.**
> 행복에서 불행까지는 한 발짝밖에 안 되지만, 불행에서 행복까지는 멀다.

From fortune to misfortune is but a step; from misfortune to fortunes a long way.

● 나도 작가처럼

You were born together, and together you
shall be forevermore.
You shall be together when the white
wings of death scatter your days.
Ay, you shall be together even in the
silent memory of God.

그대들은 함께 태어났고, 또 영원히 함께할 것입니다.
죽음의 흰 날개가 그대들의 삶의 날을 흩어버릴 때에도 그대들은 함께 있을 것입니다.
정녕 그렇습니다. 신의 고요한 기억 속에서조차도 그대들은 함께 있을 것입니다.
(칼릴 지브란, '예언자' - 결혼에 대하여)

필기체 대문자와 소문자를 써보세요.

V $\mathcal{V}$ $\mathcal{u}$

$\mathcal{V}$

$\mathcal{u}$

$\mathcal{V}$ $\mathcal{u}$

속담과 격언속에서 만나는 단어

vast 광대한

vast   vast

Books are ships which pass through the vast seas of time.
책이란 광대한 시간의 바다를 지나가는 배이다.

Books are ships which pass through the vast seas of time.

vengeance 복수

vengeance   vengeance

Heaven's vengeance is slow but sure.
하늘의 복수는 더디지만 확실하다.

Heaven's vengeance is slow but sure.

venture 모험

venture   venture

Life is venture or nothing.
인생은 모험이거나 아무것도 아닌 것이다.

Life is venture or nothing.

victory 승리

victory   victory

Tighten your helmet strings in victory.
승리했을 때 투구 끈을 졸라매라.

Tighten your helmet strings in victory.

vision 비전, 선견지명

vision   vision

A man of vision will make good in the end.
비전이 있는 사람은 결국 성공한다.

A man of vision will make good in the end.

명언 여행

Work banishes those three great evils, boredom, vice and poverty.
노동은 지루함, 부도덕 그리고 가난이라는 세 개의 큰 악을 제거한다.

Work banishes those three great evils, boredom,

vice and poverty.

Never give up. Today is hard, tomorrow will be worse, but the day after tomorrow will be sunshine.
절대 포기하지 마라. 오늘은 힘들고, 내일은 더 안 좋아질 것이다. 하지만 모레는 햇빛이 비칠 것이다.

Never give up. Today is hard, tomorrow will be worse,

but the day after tomorrow will be sunshine.

In the morning of life, work; in the midday, give counsel; in the evening, pray.
인생의 아침에는 일을 하고, 낮에는 조언하며, 저녁에는 기도하라.

In the morning of life, work; in the midday,

give counsel; in the evening, pray.

● 나도 작가처럼

In my younger and more vulnerable years my father gave me some advice that I've been turning over in my mind ever since.
"Whenever you feel like criticizing anyone," he told me, "just remember that all the people in this world haven't had the advantages that you've had."

내가 어려서 쉽게 상처를 받았던 시절 아버지께서 충고로 해준 말이 있다. 그 이후로 나는 이 말씀을 마음속에 되새기고 있다. "누구를 비난하고 싶거든," 아버지께서 내게 말씀하셨다. "먼저 떠올리거라. 네가 일찍이 누려온 혜택들을 누구나 받은 것은 아니라는 사실을 말이다." (피츠제럴드 '위대한 개츠비' - 첫 문장)

In my younger and more vulnerable years my father
gave me some advice that I've been turning over
in my mind ever since.
"Whenever you feel like criticizing anyone," he told me,
"just remember that all the people in this world haven't
had the advantages that you've had."

필기체 대문자와 소문자를 써보세요.

W W w

_W_

_w_

_W w_

속담과 격언속에서 만나는 단어

wait 기다리다

wait wait

Time and tide wait for no man.
세월은 사람을 기다리지 않는다.

Time and tide wait for no man.

wake 깨우다

wake wake

Wake not a sleeping lion.
잠자는 사자를 깨우지 마라.

Wake not a sleeping lion.

weak 약한

weak weak

Weak things united become strong.
약한 것도 합치면 강해진다.

Weak things united become strong.

whole 전체의

whole whole

Woman's whole life is a history of love.
여성의 일생은 사랑의 역사이다.

Woman's whole life is a history of love.

will 의지, 뜻

will will

Where there's a will, there's a way.
뜻이 있는 곳에 길이 있다.

Where there's a will, there's a way.

명언 여행

When wealth is lost, nothing is lost; when health is lost, something is lost; when character is lost, all is lost.

부를 잃으면 아무것도 잃지 않은 것이고, 건강을 잃으면 조금 잃는 것이고, 성품을 잃으면 모든 것을 잃는 것이다.

When wealth is lost, nothing is lost; when health is lost, something is lost; when character is lost, all is lost.

In her first passion a woman loves her lover, in all the others all she loves is love.

여자는 첫사랑에서 연인을 사랑하지만, 그 나머지 사랑에선 사랑 그 자체를 사랑한다.

In her first passion a woman loves her lover, in all the others all she loves is love.

When you talk, you only repeat what you know. But if you listen, you may learn something new.

당신이 이야기를 할 때는 자신이 아는 것만 반복하게 되지만, 만약 듣는다면 당신은 새로운 것을 배울 수 있을 것이다.

When you talk, you only repeat what you know. But if you listen, you may learn something new.

● 나도 작가처럼

It was the best of times,
it was the worst of times,
it was the age of wisdom,
it was the age of foolishness,
it was the epoch of belief,
it was the epoch of incredulity.

최고의 시절이었고, 또한 최악의 시절이었다.
지혜의 시기였고, 또한 어리석음의 시기였다.
믿음의 시대였고, 또한 불신의 시대였다.
(찰스 디킨스 '두 도시 이야기' - 첫 문장)

It was the best of times,

it was the worst of times,

it was the age of wisdom,

it was the age of foolishness,

it was the epoch of belief,

it was the epoch of incredulity.

○ 필기체 대문자와 소문자를 써보세요.

X x

Xx

● 속담과 격언속에서 만나는 단어

Xmas 크리스마스

Xmas Xmas

Xmas(X-mas) is a common abbreviation of the word Christmas.
Xmas는 일반적으로 크리스마스(Christmas)라는 단어의 약자이다.

Xmas(X-mas) is a common abbreviation of the word Christmas.

X-ray 엑스선

X-ray X-ray

X-ray imaging creates pictures of the inside of your body.
엑스선 영상은 당신 몸의 내부 사진을 만들어 낸다.

X-ray imaging creates pictures of the inside of your body.

● 필기체 대문자와 소문자를 써보세요.

● 속담과 격언속에서 만나는 단어

yield 산출하다, 내다

yield   yield

A tree with beautiful blossoms does not always yield the best fruit.
아름다운 꽃을 피우는 나무가 늘 최고의 열매를 맺는 건 아니다.

A tree with beautiful blossoms does not always yield the best fruit.

young 젊은

young   young

The owl thinks her own young fairest.
올빼미도 제 새끼가 가장 예쁘다고 생각한다.

The owl thinks her own young fairest.

필기체 대문자와 소문자를 써보세요.

속담과 격언속에서 만나는 단어

zeal 열의, 열중

zeal zeal

Zeal without knowledge is fanaticism.
지식이 없이 열중하는 것은 광신이다.

Zeal without knowledge is fanaticism.

zest 열정

zest zest

Zest is the secret of all beauty.
열정은 모든 아름다움의 비밀이다.

Zest is the secret of all beauty.

You have your way. I have my way. As for the right way, the correct way, and the only way, it does not exist.

당신에게는 당신의 길이 있고 내게는 나의 길이 있다. 옳은 길, 똑바른 길, 유일한 길에 대해서 말하자면, 그런 것들은 존재하지 않는다.

You have your way. I have my way. As for the right way,
the correct way, and the only way, it does not exist.

If you want to know where you are going to be five years from now, listen to your words.

지금부터 5년 후에 당신이 어디에 있을지 알고 싶다면, 당신의 말에 귀를 기울여보라.

If you want to know where you are going to be
five years from now, listen to your words.

In today's hurried technology-driven society, Zoom Focus is more important than ever.

오늘날의 급속한 기술중심의 사회에서는 줌 포커스(작은 일에 집중하는 것)가 어느 때 보다 더 중요하다.

In today's hurried technology-driven society,
Zoom Focus is more important than ever.

107

명언 여행

It is a truth universally acknowledged, that a single man in possession of a good fortune,
must be in want of a wife.
However, little known the feelings or views of such a man may be on his first entering a neighbourhood,
this truth is so well fixed in the minds of the surrounding families, that he is considered the rightful property of someone or other of their daughters.

재산깨나 있는 독신자에게 아내가 있어야 한다는 것은 누구나 인정하는 진리다.
이런 남자가 이웃이 되면 그 사람의 감정이나 생각에 대해 거의 아는 바가 없다고 해도,
이 진리가 동네 사람들의 마음속에 너무나 확고하게 자리 잡고 있기 때문에,
자기네 딸 중에서 누군가 그를 차지할 정당한 권리가 있다고 생각하기 마련이다.
(제인 오스틴 '오만과 편견' - 첫 문장)

It is a truth universally acknowledged, that a single
man in possession of a good fortune,
must be in want of a wife.
However, little known the feelings or views of such
a man may be on his first entering a neighbourhood,
this truth is so well fixed in the minds of the
surrounding families, that he is considered the
rightful property of someone or other of their daughters.

인생에
한 번쯤은 필기체로
영어 써보기

My Cursive
Handwriting Book

a b c d e f g h i j k l m n o p q r s t u v w x y z

small letters

A B C D E F G H I J K L M N O P Q R S T U V W X Y Z

capital letters

My Cursive
Handwriting Book

인생에
한 번쯤은 필기체로
영어 써보기